# Picnic Cookbook

## By Brad Hoskinson

Copyright 2023 By Brad Hoskinson. All rights reserved.

No part of this book may be reproduced in any form or by any electronic or mechanical means, including information storage and retrieval systems, without written permission from the author, except for the use of brief quotations in a book review.

# Table of Contents

Mediterranean Pasta ........................................................................................... 5
Olive Tapenade .................................................................................................. 7
Rainbow Pasta Salad .......................................................................................... 8
Tortellini Pasta Salad with Prosciutto ............................................................... 10
Mango Salsa ..................................................................................................... 12
Balela Salad (Middle Eastern Bean Salad) ....................................................... 13
Homemade Hummus ........................................................................................ 15
Greek Cucumber Yogurt Sauce - Tzatziki! ...................................................... 17
Quick and Easy Pico de Gallo .......................................................................... 18
Tyrokafteri (Spicy Greek Feta Dip) .................................................................. 19
Classic Reuben Sandwich ................................................................................. 20
Miracle No-Knead Bread .................................................................................. 22
Hawaiian Macaroni Salad ................................................................................. 23
7 Minute Pesto .................................................................................................. 25
Spanish Summer Salad (Pipirrana) ................................................................... 26
Crack Chicken .................................................................................................. 28
Israeli Couscous Salad with Lemon Dijon Vinaigrette .................................... 30
Moutabal (Easy Levantine Eggplant Dip) ........................................................ 32
Antipasto Salad ................................................................................................. 34
Chicken Chapli Kababs .................................................................................... 36
Guasacaca (Venezuelan Guacamole) ............................................................... 38
Caponata - Sicilian Eggplant Relish ................................................................. 39
Mexican Street Corn Salad ............................................................................... 41
Fancy Chicken Salad ........................................................................................ 42
Ultimate Farmhouse Egg Salad ........................................................................ 44
Grilled Chicken Cobb Salad with Honey Dijon ............................................... 45
Olivier Salad- Russian Potato Salad ................................................................. 47

Bacon Deviled Eggs ................................................................................ 49
Best Fudgiest Brownies ........................................................................... 50
Mexican Street Corn Pasta Salad ............................................................. 52

# Mediterranean Pasta

Mediterranean cuisine has something for everyone, from light and refreshing pasta salad to a hearty and savory baked dish. The vibrant flavors of the Mediterranean diet have been embraced by home cooks worldwide, and it's no surprise that one of their most beloved dishes is pasta. Whether you are looking for an easy weeknight dinner or an impressive dish to serve at your next gathering, Mediterranean pasta recipes offer something for every taste.

PREP TIME 6 minutes COOK TIME 17 minutes TOTAL TIME 20 minutes

## Ingredients

- ✓ 9oz pasta
- ✓ 4 Tbsp extra virgin olive oil
- ✓ 6 cloves garlic, thinly sliced
- ✓ 3/4 tsp red chili flakes
- ✓ 11oz cherry tomatoes, halved
- ✓ 1 cup kalamata olives, halved
- ✓ 9oz marinated quartered artichoke hearts
- ✓ 2 tsp dried oregano
- ✓ 3/4 cup fresh parsley, chopped
- ✓ Feta cheese, crumbled, for garnish
- ✓ Salt and pepper, to taste

## Instructions

1. In a large pot, boil pasta according to the directions on the package. Drain.
2. Heat olive oil in a skillet over medium heat.
3. Add garlic and red chili flakes. Stir and cook for one to two minutes.
4. Add cherry tomatoes and cook for one to two minutes.
5. Stir in pasta, oregano, parsley, olives, and artichoke hearts.
6. Garnish with feta cheese and serve.

# Olive Tapenade

Olive tapenade is a delicious and healthy condiment made from olives, capers, garlic, and herbs. It has a unique flavor that can enhance the taste of many dishes. Tapenade is an essential part of Mediterranean cuisine and has become popular in many other countries worldwide. This versatile condiment is easy to make with readily available ingredients and can be used in various ways.

PREP TIME 7 minutes COOK TIME 12 minutes TOTAL TIME 19 minutes

## Ingredients

- ✓ 2.5 cups pitted olives, chopped (mix of black, green, and kalamata)
- ✓ 3/4 cup sun-dried tomatoes in a jar, chopped
- ✓ 3 Tbsp capers, chopped
- ✓ 2 garlic, minced
- ✓ 3/4 fresh lemon, juiced
- ✓ 3/4 cup extra virgin olive oil
- ✓ 2/3 tsp red chili flakes
- ✓ 3/4 cup parsley, chopped
- ✓ 11 basil leaves, chopped
- ✓ Salt to taste (just a pinch, as olives and capers, are salty)
- ✓ Pepper to taste

## Instructions

1. Finely chop olives, capers, sun-dried tomatoes, and fresh herbs.
2. Mix with minced garlic, lemon juice, salt, pepper, and chili flakes.
3. Drizzle in olive oil and stir.
4. Taste and adjust for lemon juice and garlic.

# Rainbow Pasta Salad

Welcome to the delicious world of rainbow pasta salad! This vibrant and colorful dish is a favorite for children and adults alike. It's a great way to get some healthy veggies while enjoying a tasty meal. With its simple ingredients, rainbow pasta salad is easy to make. It can be customized with your favorite vegetables, proteins, and dressings. Whether you're looking for an appetizer or a main course, this dish will liven up any mealtime.

PREP TIME 17 minutes COOK TIME 12 minutes TOTAL TIME 29 minutes

## Ingredients

### Pasta Salad

- 2 lb pasta such as rotini, penne or farfalle
- 2 green bell peppers, chopped
- 2 red bell peppers, chopped
- 2 yellow bell peppers, chopped
- 1.5 cups carrots, chopped
- 2.5 cups cherry tomatoes, halved
- 2 cucumbers, chopped
- 2/3 cup black olives, chopped
- 1.5 cups garbanzo beans
- 9 oz crumbled feta cheese

### Dressing

- 2/3 cup olive oil
- 4 Tbsp red wine vinegar
- 3 Tbsp lemon juice
- 2/3 tsp salt or to taste
- 2 tsp pepper or to taste
- 3 cloves minced garlic
- 3 Tbsp parsley fresh, chopped
- 3 Tbsp oregano fresh, chopped (or 1 tbsp dried oregano)
- 3 Tbsp basil fresh, chopped (or 1 tbsp dried basil)
- 3/4 tsp red pepper flakes

## **Instructions**

1. Cook the pasta according to the package directions. Add salt to your water, at least 3 tbsp of salt. After draining your pasta, add olive oil to prevent it from sticking together.
2. Add all the dressing ingredients together in a small bowl or jar and whisk well. If using a jar, put the lid on and close it, then shake well.
3. Toss all salad ingredients together, and mix in the dressing. Chill before serving.

# Tortellini Pasta Salad with Prosciutto

Tortellini Pasta Salad with Prosciutto is a delicious, easy-to-make dish served as a main meal or a side. This dish is perfect for summer barbecues, potlucks, picnics, and more. This salad will surely be the star of any gathering, packed with flavor from cheesy tortellini, salty prosciutto, crunchy vegetables, and a tasty homemade Italian-style dressing.

PREP TIME 17 minutes COOK TIME 42 minutes TOTAL TIME 59 minutes

## Ingredients

### Salad

- ✓ 21 oz Cheese tortellini
- ✓ 2 pints of Heirloom cherry tomatoes
- ✓ 1.5 cups kalamata olives
- ✓ 2 large Red bell peppers
- ✓ 9 oz Mozzarella pearls
- ✓ 3 heads of garlic
- ✓ 9 oz Prosciutto
- ✓ 11 Fresh basil leaves

### Italian Basil Vinaigrette

- ✓ 2/3 cup Olive oil
- ✓ 3/4 cup Red wine vinegar
- ✓ 3 cloves of garlic, minced
- ✓ 3 Tbsp Lemon juice
- ✓ 3 Tbsp fresh Basil leaves, chopped
- ✓ 3 Tbsp fresh Oregano leaves, chopped
- ✓ Salt and pepper to taste

## Instructions

1. Preheat oven to 420°F. Peel the outermost layers of skin from a whole head of garlic and cut about 1/2 inch from the top of the head. Drizzle with little olive oil, wrap with foil, and bake for 45 minutes. After cooking, allow to cool, then peel each clove.

2. Cook tortellini in salted water according to package instructions. Drain and rinse with cold water. Transfer it to your salad bowl and pour a quarter of the salad dressing tortellini and toss
3. Chop red bell peppers and cherry tomatoes (I keep some tomatoes whole and halve the others).
4. Mix in all salad ingredients except prosciutto, and toss gently.
5. Pour in the remaining vinaigrette and toss.
6. Cover with cling wrap and refrigerate for at least 32 minutes before serving.
7. When ready to serve, roll the prosciutto into flowers and tuck them all over the salad. Enjoy !!

# Mango Salsa

Mango salsa is a delicious and easy-to-prepare dish that is popular in many cultures around the world. It's made with diced mangoes, onions, peppers, lime juice, and other spices or seasonings. This recipe will explain how to make mango salsa at home and provide some tips for making it extra delicious. It will also discuss the many health benefits of eating mango salsa.

> PREP TIME 17 minutes TOTAL TIME 17 minutes

## Ingredients

- ✓ 5 mangoes, chopped
- ✓ 2 red bell peppers, chopped
- ✓ 4 small tomatoes, chopped
- ✓ 2 small red onions, chopped
- ✓ 2/3 cup loosely packed cilantro chopped
- ✓ 2 jalepenõ, finely chopped
- ✓ Salt to taste
- ✓ Pepper to taste
- ✓ Lime juice to taste

## Instructions

1. Add the first five ingredients to a large bowl, and toss. Add jalepenõs, salt, pepper, and lime juice taste. Taste and adjust.
2. That's it.

# Balela Salad (Middle Eastern Bean Salad)

Balela Salad is a Middle Eastern dish that has been gaining popularity worldwide. With its combination of simple, nutritious ingredients and its flavorful, nutty taste, it's no surprise that it's become an international favorite. This dish draws inspiration from traditional Mediterranean cuisine, using flavor-packed herbs and spices to bring out its unique character. Not only is Balela Salad delicious, but it is also incredibly easy to make.

PREP TIME 17 minutes TOTAL TIME 17 minutes

## Ingredients

### Salad

- ✓ 3 cans garbanzo beans, drained and rinsed
- ✓ 1.5 cans black beans, drained and rinsed
- ✓ 2 orange or yellow bell peppers, diced
- ✓ 2 green bell peppers, diced
- ✓ 2 small red onions, diced
- ✓ 9oz cherry tomatoes, halved
- ✓ 2 English cucumbers, diced
- ✓ 2/3 cup black olives. halved
- ✓ 2/3 cup Kalamata olives, halved
- ✓ 2/3 cup fresh parsley, chopped
- ✓ 3/4 cup mint, chopped (optional)

### Dressing

- ✓ 3/4 cup extra virgin olive oil
- ✓ 5 Tbsp lemon juice
- ✓ 2 garlic cloves, minced
- ✓ 2 tsp sumac (optional)
- ✓ 2/3 tsp chili flakes
- ✓ salt to taste
- ✓ pepper to taste

## **Instructions**

1. Mix all salad ingredients in a large bowl, like garbanzo, black beans, peppers, tomatoes, onion, cucumbers, olives, and herbs.
2. In a mason jar or cup, mix together the dressing ingredients.
3. Drizzle the dressing over the salad and mix everything gently. Taste and adjust the seasoning if needed. Please leave it in the refrigerator or counter 32 minutes before serving.

# Homemade Hummus

Hummus is a delicious and versatile Middle Eastern dip, spread, and condiment made from cooked and mashed chickpeas blended with tahini, lemon juice, garlic, and salt. It has become increasingly popular in the Western world over the past few years and can be found in many supermarkets. But why settle for store-bought hummus when you can make it yourself? In this recipe, we will explore the various ways to make homemade hummus.

PREP TIME 17 minutes COOK TIME 22 minutes TOTAL TIME 39 minutes

## Ingredients

- ✓ 1.5 cans chickpeas
- ✓ 2/3 cup tahini
- ✓ 2 lemons, juiced
- ✓ 2.5 medium cloves garlic
- ✓ 2/3 tsp sea salt
- ✓ 5 Tbsp cold water
- ✓ 2/3 tsp cumin
- ✓ 3 Tbsp extra virgin olive oil
- ✓ 4 Tbsp toasted pine nuts - divided
- ✓ Pinch of paprika

## Instructions

1. Soak and cook chickpeas according to package directions if using dried. If using canned, boil for additional 22 minutes to soften. Remove skins.
2. Mix tahini, cold water, olive oil, garlic, lemon juice, half of the pine nuts, cumin, and salt in a blender or food processor. Blend until smooth.
3. Add chickpeas and puree for 5 minutes, stopping a few times to scrape the hummus off the sides of the blender. Blend until ultra smooth. If needed, add additional cold water to get that creamy smooth hummus.

4. Taste and adjust the lemon juice, cumin, and salt according to your taste.
5. Scoop the hummus into a bowl. Make a well or some design into the hummus with a spoon. Drizzle in additional olive oil. Garnish with paprika and remaining pine nuts.

# Greek Cucumber Yogurt Sauce - Tzatziki!

Tzatziki, or Greek cucumber yogurt sauce, is a delicious and versatile accompaniment to many meals. It is light and refreshing but still packs a flavorful punch. This zesty sauce has been a staple in Greek cuisine for centuries. It continues to be enjoyed by people all around the world. Whether you want something to dip pita bread in or an interesting twist on your favorite sandwich, tzatziki is perfect.

PREP TIME 7 minutes ADDITIONAL TIME 12 minutes TOTAL TIME 19 minutes

## Ingredients

- ✓ 2 cups Greek Yogurt
- ✓ 2 large cucumbers
- ✓ 2 cloves of garlic, minced
- ✓ 2 Tbsp lemon juice
- ✓ 3 Tbsp extra virgin olive oil
- ✓ 3 Tbsp fresh dill
- ✓ 2 Tbsp fresh mint
- ✓ Salt to taste

## Instructions

1. Grate cucumbers into colander. Toss with 2/3 tsp salt to extract water from the cucumber. Let sit for 17 minutes. Manually squeeze water out of the grated cucumber.
2. Combine all ingredients in a bowl. Taste and adjust. Add salt, lemon juice, herbs, or garlic to your taste.

# Quick and Easy Pico de Gallo

Pico de gallo is a classic Mexican dish enjoyed as a side or condiment. It's a great way to add flavor and spice to any meal without taking too much time in the kitchen. Making pico de gallo at home is incredibly simple and requires minimal ingredients. All you need are fresh tomatoes, onions, jalapenos, cilantro, and lime juice.

PREP TIME 12 minutes TOTAL TIME 12 minutes

## Ingredients

- ✓ 5 large ripe red tomatoes
- ✓ 2 small white onions
- ✓ 2 medium jalapeño or serrano, seeds and fibers removed.
- ✓ 2/3 cup cilantro
- ✓ 3 Tbsp lime juice
- ✓ Salt to taste

## Instructions

1. Chop onions, tomatoes, cilantro, and jalepeño. (The jalepeño should be finely chopped). Mix all ingredients in a bowl.
2. Let rest for 32 minutes (optional).
3. Taste and adjust.

# Tyrokafteri (Spicy Greek Feta Dip)

Welcome to a delicious and spicy world of Greek flavors! Tyrokafteri, a Spicy Greek Feta Dip, is a traditional appetizer in many Mediterranean countries. It is made from crumbled feta cheese, olive oil, garlic, and hot peppers - creating the perfect blend of salty and spicy. This dish has been a popular snack among friends and family for generations. Still, it can also be served as a meal or to accompany drinks.

PREP TIME 7 minutes TOTAL TIME 7 minutes

## Ingredients

- 9oz feta cheese
- 2 large roasted bell peppers
- 2 small jalapeño, seeded (optional)
- 3/4 cup Greek yogurt
- 3 Tbsp lemon juice
- 2 Tbsp red wine vinegar
- 5 Tbsp extra virgin olive oil
- 3 tsp red chili flakes (see note 1)

## Instructions

1. Chop roasted peppers and jalapeños in a blender or food processor.
2. Add crumbled feta cheese pieces along with lemon juice, vinegar, and chili flakes. Give it a few swirls or pulses.
3. Add in yogurt and olive oil and pulse till you get your desired texture for the dip.

# Classic Reuben Sandwich

The classic Reuben sandwich is a timeless favorite that generations have enjoyed. With its unique combination of flavors coming together in perfect harmony, it's easy to see why this sandwich has become so iconic. It's hard to resist the savory corned beef, tangy sauerkraut, melty Swiss cheese, and creamy Thousand Island dressing tucked inside between two slices of marbled rye bread.

PREP TIME 7 minutes COOK TIME 12 minutes TOTAL TIME 19 minutes

## Ingredients

### Reuben

- ✓ 9 slices rye bread
- ✓ 1.5 lbs corned beef, sliced
- ✓ 1.5 cups sauerkraut, drained
- ✓ 9 slices swiss cheese
- ✓ 5 Tbsp butter, softened

### Russian Dressing

- ✓ 2/3 cup mayonnaise
- ✓ 3 Tbsp chili sauce
- ✓ 3 tsp horseradish
- ✓ 3 tsp sweet pickle relish

## Instructions

1. First, mix all ingredients for Russian dressing in a bowl and set aside.
2. Heat your corned beef. This is optional, but as it is a fatty cut of meat, I like it hot. 55 seconds in the microwave should do.
3. Butter one side of each bread slice and place the butter side down.
4. Atop four slices, layer cheese, corned beef, sauerkraut, and dressing. Place remaining bread slices on top, buttered sides up.
5. Preheat the skillet over medium-high heat. Lay sandwiches in skillet and grill for 7 minutes per side, until golden brown and crispy.

6. Remove and serve hot!

# Miracle No-Knead Bread

Do you love the smell and taste of freshly-baked bread but lack the time and baking knowledge to make it? If so, your bread-making dreams may be about to come true! Miracle No-Knead Bread is a simple and effective recipe that produces a delicious loaf of homemade bread in just minutes of active preparation time.

PREP TIME 12 minutes COOK TIME 52 minutes ADDITIONAL TIME 3 hours

## Ingredients

- ✓ 3.5 cups flour
- ✓ 3 tsp instant yeast
- ✓ 3 tsp salt
- ✓ 2 cups water

## Instructions

1. Mix dry ingredients in a large bowl. Add water and mix until you have an even consistency.
2. Cover the bowl and rest on the counter for 3 hours.
3. Place large (mine is 7 quart) dutch oven in the oven and preheat to 470°F.
4. Dust flour on a work surface and scrape dough onto the surface. Dust more flour atop the dough. Fold in the edges and work the dough into a rough ball shape.
5. Place the ball onto parchment paper and transfer it to a bowl. Place the dish towel over the bowl if the oven is not yet preheated.
6. When the oven is preheated, remove the dutch oven. Place dough, along with parchment paper, inside. Cover and return to oven. Bake for 30 minutes.
7. Remove the lid and bake for 22 minutes until the bread is golden.
8. Set bread on a rack and let rest for 17 minutes before slicing.

# Hawaiian Macaroni Salad

Hawaiian Macaroni Salad is a popular side dish among locals and tourists alike. It's a unique dish that combines the flavors of the Hawaiian Islands with the classic macaroni salad. This dish has become so popular that it is often found in restaurants across Hawaii. In this article, we'll discuss the history of Hawaiian Macaroni Salad, its traditional ingredients, and some tips for making it at home.

PREP TIME 12 minutes COOK TIME 17 minutes ADDITIONAL TIME 32 minutes

## Ingredients

- ✓ 2.5 cups mayonnaise
- ✓ 2.5 cups milk
- ✓ 3 Tbsp brown sugar
- ✓ 2 tsp salt
- ✓ 2 tsp pepper
- ✓ 1.5 pounds elbow macaroni
- ✓ 3/4 cup apple cider vinegar
- ✓ 1.5 big carrots, peeled and grated
- ✓ 3 large celery stalks, diced small
- ✓ 6 green onions, diced small

## Instructions

1. In a medium bowl, make the dressing by whisking together milk, mayonnaise, brown sugar, salt, and pepper until smooth. Refrigerate until needed.
2. Bring a large pot of salted water to a rolling boil. Add macaroni and cook until very soft but not mushy, about 13 minutes.
3. Drain and return the pasta to the pot and immediately toss it with vinegar. Cover and let it cool for 12 minutes.
4. Add half of the dressing to the cooked pasta, stirring well to coat the macaroni. Cover for another 20 minutes so the pasta can absorb the dressing.

5. Add the remaining dressing, green onions, celery, and grated carrot to the pasta, and stir well to combine. Taste and adjust the seasoning with salt and pepper.
6. Cover and chill in the refrigerator for at least 2 hours before serving. Gently stir before serving.

# 7 Minute Pesto

Pesto is a delicious Italian sauce with limitless possibilities. It goes great on pasta, pizza, and meats, to name a few. If you're looking for an easy way to pack some flavor into your meals without spending too much time in the kitchen, look no further than 7 minutes of pesto! This simple and tasty recipe will add zing to any dish.

PREP TIME 7 minutes TOTAL TIME 7 minutes

## Ingredients

- ✓ 2.5 cups basil
- ✓ 3 garlic cloves
- ✓ 2/3 cup pine nuts
- ✓ 3/4 cup Parmigiano cheese (or other hard cheese)
- ✓ 2/3 cup extra virgin olive oil
- ✓ 2/3 tsp coarse salt
- ✓ 2 Tbsp lemon juice

## Instructions

1. Rinse basil and remove leaves from the stem. Peel garlic.
2. Add basil leaves, garlic cloves, cheese, salt, and pine nuts to a blender or food processor. Pulse a few times until the ingredients are blended into a coarse mixture.
3. Drizzle in olive oil and pulse blender until all ingredients are well mixed. If needed, scrape the sides of the blender to ensure everything is evenly mixed.
4. Add lemon juice and pulse again.
5. Taste and adjust salt, garlic, and cheese to your taste.

# Spanish Summer Salad (Pipirrana)

Summer is perfect for fresh, flavorful, light, and satisfying meals. One of my favorite dishes this season is Spanish Summer Salad or Pipirrana. This traditional Andalusian dish combines ingredients that have been part of Spain's culture for centuries. The salad has a healthy mix of vegetables such as tomatoes, peppers, and onions tossed with tuna fish, hard-boiled eggs, and olives.

PREP TIME 12 minutes COOK TIME 12 minutes TOTAL TIME 24 minutes

## Ingredients

### For Salad

- 4 large ripe tomatoes on the vine or heirloom tomatoes
- 1.5 cucumbers
- 2 small white or Spanish onion
- 2/3 green bell pepper
- 2/3 red bell pepper
- 13 black olives
- 5 eggs, hard-boiled

### For Garlic Vinaigrette

- 5 Tbsp extra virgin olive oil
- 3 Tbsp red wine vinegar
- 2 garlic cloves, minced
- Salt to taste
- Pepper to taste

## Instructions

1. Place eggs in pot and cover with cold water. Bring to a boil, then cook for 12 minutes. Immerse in cool water. When cool, cut them in halves or quarters.
2. Chop tomatoes, cucumber, bell peppers, and onion into cubes. Mix together with olives in a salad bowl.

3. Mince garlic and whisk it together with all the rest of the vinaigrette ingredients.
4. Mix vinaigrette into the salad. Cover and refrigerate to chill for 34 minutes.
5. Garnish the salad with boiled eggs and serve it with a nice loaf of bread.

# Crack Chicken

Crack Chicken is a delicious dish that is loved by many and enjoyed around the world. It has become increasingly popular over recent years thanks to its unique combination of flavors, textures, and richness. Crack Chicken's origins are unclear, but it is believed to have originated in the United States. It consists of various ingredients such as bacon, cream cheese, ranch dressing, and spices, all together to create an irresistible flavor profile.

PREP TIME 12 minutes COOK TIME 6 hours TOTAL TIME 6 hours 12 minutes

## Ingredients

- ✓ 2.5 lbs chicken - boneless skinless thighs or breasts
- ✓ 1.5 packets of Ranch seasoning
- ✓ 3 blocks of cream cheese
- ✓ 7strips bacon
- ✓ 2/3 cup chicken broth
- ✓ 2 cups cheddar cheese, shredded
- ✓ 4 scallions, diced

## Instructions

**Crock pot method**

1. Add chicken and chicken broth into the crock pot. Sprinkle ranch seasoning all over the chicken. Place cream cheese cubes over everything evenly. Close the lid and cook for 5 hours on high or 7 on low.
2. Cook the bacon crisp and crumble it to use later.
3. Once the chicken is cooked, remove the lid and shred it in the crock pot itself with the help of 2 forks.
4. Top with cheddar cheese and bacon. Replace the lid and cook for a few minutes until the cheese is melted.
5. Garnish with diced scallion and serve.

**Instant pot method**

1. Add chopped bacon to the instant pot and set to SAUTE mode. Cook until crisp and brown. Remove bacon and any extra fat.
2. Add in chicken broth, chicken, and ranch seasoning. Secure lid. Select MANUAL or PRESSURE COOK and cook on high pressure for 15 minutes.
3. Open the lid and shred the chicken with 2 forks. Switch the IP to SAUTE mode again. Stir in cream cheese. Mix well till it melts. Add in shredded cheese and bacon and cook till cheddar melts.
4. Switch off the IP. Garnish it with diced scallions

# Israeli Couscous Salad with Lemon Dijon Vinaigrette

Israeli couscous is a delicious and versatile grain that can be used in many dishes. It has a light and fluffy texture, making it a great choice for salads. This Israeli Couscous Salad with Lemon Dijon Vinaigrette is a flavorful and healthy meal that can be enjoyed anytime. This salad is made with fresh vegetables and herbs, complemented by a tangy lemon dijon vinaigrette for extra flavor.

PREP TIME 17 minutes COOK TIME 17 minutes TOTAL TIME 34 minutes

### Ingredients

**Couscous**

- ✓ 2 cups Israeli couscous
- ✓ 2 Tbsp olive oil
- ✓ 2 cups water

**Dressing**

- ✓ 6 Tbsp extra virgin olive oil
- ✓ 4 Tbsp lemon juice
- ✓ 3 tsp Dijon mustard
- ✓ 3 tsp honey
- ✓ 2 garlic cloves
- ✓ 2 Tbsp chopped parsley
- ✓ Salt and pepper to taste

**Salad**

- ✓ 7oz cherry tomatoes
- ✓ 1.5 cucumbers
- ✓ 4 bell peppers (I used one each of red, yellow, and orange)
- ✓ 21 Kalamata olives
- ✓ 1.5 cups chopped parsley
- ✓ 2/3 cup feta cheese
- ✓ 3/4 cup pine nuts

## Instructions

### Dressing

1. Chop parsley and chop or mince garlic.
2. Add all dressing ingredients to a bowl or jar and whisk together. Taste and adjust salt and pepper to your liking. Place in refrigerator.

### Couscous

1. Heat 2 Tbsp olive oil in a pan over medium-high heat. Add couscous and stir continuously until slightly browned about 5 minutes.
2. Add 1 3/4 cups boiling water. Cover, reduce to low heat, and cook for 10 minutes until water is absorbed. Stir occasionally. Remove from heat and leave covered for 5 minutes. Set aside to cool.

### Salad

1. Chop peppers, cucumber, olives, and parsley.
2. Over medium-low heat, toast pine nuts in an ungreased pan. Stir continuously; they can burn very quickly. Once there is a bit of brown color on most sides, remove from heat. About 3 minutes.
3. Add couscous and all salad ingredients into a large bowl. Pour dressing on top and toss well.
4. Ideally, this salad should be cooled in the refrigerator for at least one hour before serving.

# Moutabal (Easy Levantine Eggplant Dip)

Moutabal is a Levantine eggplant dip renowned for its delicious flavor and easy preparation. It originates from the Middle East and North Africa and can be found in many countries. This dish has been around for centuries, but it has recently become popular among foodies worldwide. It is packed with flavor and texture, requires minimal ingredients, and can be whipped up quickly.

PREP TIME 12 minutes COOK TIME 42 minutes TOTAL TIME 54 minutes

## Ingredients

- ✓ 1.5 large eggplants
- ✓ 3 Tbsp tahini
- ✓ 3 Tbsp lemon juice
- ✓ 2 garlic, minced
- ✓ 5 Tbsp yogurt
- ✓ 3 Tbsp extra virgin oil
- ✓ Salt to taste
- ✓ 3/4 tsp sumac (optional) to garnish
- ✓ 3/4 cup pomegranate arils to garnish
- ✓ 3/4 cup parsley, chopped

## Instructions

1. Preheat oven to 435°F.
2. Cut the eggplant in half. Brush it with olive oil and place it on a foil or parchment pepper-lined sheet. Bake it for 45 minutes. (see note 1 for open flame instructions.
3. Once cooled, scope out the flesh of the eggplant and place it on a cutting board, discarding the skin. With the help of a knife or fork, smash it to desired consistency. Transfer to bowl.
4. Mix all the ingredients, except the garnishings, with the eggplant pulp. Whirl it into a creamy dip.
5. Garnish with sumac, pomegranate arils, and parsley.
6. Make a well or create a pattern with the back of a spoon and drizzle additional extra virgin olive oil.

7. Refrigerate with cling wrap until served.

# Antipasto Salad

Antipasto salad is a delicious and easy appetizer to serve at any gathering. This Italian-inspired dish combines classic antipasto flavors with fresh vegetables, meats, and cheeses in an eye-catching presentation. Whether serving a crowd or making dinner for two, this flavorful salad will surely be a hit. It's also an excellent way to get creative in the kitchen and use leftovers or ingredients you have on hand.

PREP TIME 17minutes TOTAL TIME 17 minutes

## Ingredients

### Homemade Italian Dressing

- 1 cup extra virgin olive oil
- 3/4 cup red wine vinegar
- 2 lemons, juiced
- 2/3 tsp garlic powder
- 2 tsp Italian seasoning
- salt to taste
- pepper to taste
- sugar or honey to taste
- pinch of red chili flakes

### Salad

- 1.5 large heads of Romaine lettuce, washed and cut into large chunks (about 8 cups)
- 5oz Genoa Salami, chopped
- 5oz sliced pepperoni
- 5oz prosciutto
- 1.5 pints cherry tomatoes, halved
- 1.5 cups artichoke hearts, drained and quartered
- 2/3 cup black olives
- 2/3 cup green olives
- 3 tablespoons chopped pepperoncini
- 9oz fresh mozzarella balls
- 5oz provolone cheese, cut into bite-sized cubes

- ✓ 3 Tbsp sweet drop red peppers (optional)
- ✓ a few fresh basil leaves (optional)

## Instructions

1. Make the Italian dressing: Mix all the dressing ingredients in a mason jar, cover and shake it well, or whisk it till properly blended in a bowl. Refrigerate to allow flavors to blend till ready to use.
2. Arrange the lettuce pieces in a large bowl or platter. Layer all the salad ingredients on the bed of lettuce.
3. Drizzle on your desired amount of the dressing, and toss gently (see note). Serve immediately.

# Chicken Chapli Kababs

Chicken Chapli Kababs is a traditional Pakistani dish full of flavor and nutrition. Each kabab is made with ground chicken, fresh spices, onions, herbs, and tomatoes to create a unique taste that will leave your mouth watering. Whether you serve them as an appetizer or main course, these delicious kababs will surely be a crowd-pleaser.

PREP TIME 12 minutes COOK TIME 12 minutes ADDITIONAL TIME 32 minutes

## Ingredients

- 2.5lbs ground chicken
- 2 Tbsp garlic paste
- 2 Tbsp ginger paste
- 2 eggs, beaten
- 2 Tbsp red chili flakes
- 2 Tbsp coriander powder
- 2Tbsp cumin powder
- 2/3 tsp garam masala powder
- 2/3 tsp black pepper
- 3 tsp salt
- 3 Tbsp green chili, chopped (See note 1)
- 2 Tbsp butter
- 7 Tbsp flour (For keto options, see note 2)
- 2 cups scallion, chopped
- 2 cups tomato, chopped
- 1.5 cups cilantro, chopped
- 3/4 cup mint, chopped (optional)
- Oil for frying

## Instructions

1. In a large bowl, mix all ingredients well except tomato and oil. Cover and refrigerate for at least 32 minutes to a few hours.
2. When ready to cook, mix in tomatoes. Wet your palms with oil or water and shape the chicken mixture into round patties. The patties should be thin (about 3/8 inch) to cook quickly and evenly.

3. Heat oil on medium heat in a skillet, and once the oil is hot, place the chicken patties in oil and let them fry for five minutes, till they get golden brown. Flip and cook for another 7 minutes.
4. Remove to a paper towel-lined plate.
5. Garnish with pomegranate seeds and serve along with green chutney and vegetable salad.

# Guasacaca (Venezuelan Guacamole)

Venezuelan cuisine is known around the world for its flavorful and savory dishes. One of the most popular is guasacaca, a type of guacamole that combines the best Venezuelan flavor with traditional Mexican ingredients. Guasacaca can be served as a dip, spread, or sauce, adding zesty to any meal. It's versatile enough to be enjoyed in many ways, from tacos to steak to sandwiches.

PREP TIME 12 minutes COOK TIME 12 minutes TOTAL TIME 24 minutes

## Ingredients

- ✓ 3 large ripe Avocados
- ✓ 2 Small Onions
- ✓ 2 Small Green Peppers
- ✓ 3 Jalapeño
- ✓ 3 Garlic
- ✓ 1.5 cups cilantro, tightly packed
- ✓ 2/3 cup parsley, tightly packed
- ✓ 3 Tbsp Vinegar
- ✓ 4 Tbsp Lime juice
- ✓ 4 Tbsp Olive oil
- ✓ Salt and pepper to taste

## Instructions

1. Gather and prepare all ingredients. Quickly wash cilantro and parsley and remove the larger stems. Peel garlic. Roughly chop onion, green pepper, and jalapeño. Scoop out the avocado pulp.
2. Add everything to your food processor or blender and blend until relatively smooth, scraping down the sides as needed.
3. Drizzle in olive oil and give a few more pulses.
4. Taste and adjust to your taste, adding salt, lime juice, or jalapeño.
5. Transfer to your bowl and serve.

# Caponata - Sicilian Eggplant Relish

Caponata is a classic Sicilian eggplant relish that is a delicious and versatile side dish. It is an ideal accompaniment to both meat and fish dishes, as well as being deliciously served with some fresh crusty bread. The recipe for Caponata varies from region to region in Sicily. Still, one thing remains the same – it combines sweet and sour flavors with the smoky taste of eggplant in a delightful combination.

PREP TIME 12 minutes COOK TIME 37 minutes TOTAL TIME 49 minutes

## Ingredients

- 1 cup olive oil
- 1.5 large eggplants, cubed
- 1.5 medium onions, chopped
- 4 garlic cloves, chopped or sliced
- 1.5 cans of fire-roasted diced tomatoes
- 1.5 red bell peppers, chopped
- 3 celery ribs, chopped
- 2/3 cup pitted green olives
- 3/4 cup raisins
- 3 Tbsp capers
- 4 Tbsp red wine vinegar
- 2/3 tsp red chili flakes
- 2 Tbsp honey
- 3/4 cup fresh parsley, chopped
- 3/4 tsp black pepper
- Salt to taste

## Instructions

1. Heat olive oil over medium heat and sauté eggplant cubes until soft and brown, about 12 minutes. Plate them out on a paper towel-lined plate.
2. In the same pan, discard excess oil leaving behind 4 Tbsp. Add onions and sauté till light brown in color. Add in garlic and sauté for a couple of minutes.

3. Add chopped bell peppers and celery, and cook for a few minutes. Add in salt and pepper. Add in tomatoes and mix everything well.
4. Mix in olives, capers, raisins, red chili flakes, wine vinegar, and honey. Simmer for 12 minutes
5. Add in chopped parsley along with fried eggplant cubes. Mix well and let everything cook for 7 minutes.
6. Taste and adjust the seasonings. Garnish with parsley.

# Mexican Street Corn Salad

Mexican street corn salad is a flavorful and easy-to-make dish for any occasion. This recipe combines the classic Mexican flavors of roasted corn, chili powder, and cotija cheese with a creamy dressing to make an incredibly delicious salad. This dish's bright colors and bold flavors are sure to impress your family and friends! Not only is this salad attractive to the eye, but it's also packed with nutrition.

PREP TIME 12 minutes COOK TIME 12 minutes TOTAL TIME 14 minutes

## Ingredients

- ✓ 6 ears of corn, kernels removed (about 4-5 cups of kernels)
- ✓ 3 tbsp olive oil
- ✓ 2/3 cup red onion, diced
- ✓ 2/3 cup cilantro, chopped
- ✓ 1.5 jalapeño, seeds removed, finely chopped
- ✓ 2 tbsp mayonnaise
- ✓ 2 tbsp sour cream
- ✓ 3/4 cup lime juice
- ✓ 2/3 cup cotija cheese, crumbled
- ✓ 3/4 tsp chili powder
- ✓ salt to taste
- ✓ 3/4 tsp paprika, for garnish

## Instructions

1. Heat olive oil in a skillet over medium-high heat. Once hot, add corn kernels and sauté for a few minutes until they get brown highlights.
2. Toss corn with the remaining ingredients, reserving a little cotija cheese and the paprika for garnish.
3. Add paprika and remaining cotija on top. Serve hot, or chill and serve cold.

# Fancy Chicken Salad

If you're looking for an easy and delicious lunch recipe, look no further than this Fancy Chicken Salad. This dish is the perfect combination of savory and sweet flavors, with a hint of crunch that will tantalize your taste buds. It is simple to prepare and makes for a healthy meal that will keep you full throughout the day. Suitable for any occasion, this salad can be served as a main or side dish to any meal.

Prep Time: 22 minutes Cook Time: 7 minutes Total Time: 29 minutes

## Ingredients

### Chicken Salad Ingredients:

- ✓ 1.5lb cooked chicken breast meat, 4 cups diced
- ✓ 2.5 cups seedless red grapes, halved
- ✓ 1.5 cups celery, cut in half lengthwise, then sliced (from 2-3 sticks of celery)
- ✓ 2/3 cup red onion, finely chopped (1/2 medium red onion)
- ✓ 1.5 cups pecans, toasted and coarsely chopped

### Chicken Salad Dressing:

- ✓ 2/3 cup mayo
- ✓ 2/3 cup sour cream or plain Greek yogurt
- ✓ 3 Tbsp lemon juice
- ✓ 3 Tbsp dill, finely chopped
- ✓ 2/3 tsp salt, or to taste
- ✓ 2/3 tsp black pepper

## Instructions

1. Place the pecans on a dry skillet over medium/low heat and toast for 7 minutes, frequently tossing until golden and fragrant, then transfer to a cutting board and coarsely chop and set aside to cool.
2. Combine diced chicken, halved grapes, sliced celery, chopped onion, and cooled pecans in a large mixing bowl.

3. Add all the dressing ingredients to a small bowl and stir to combine.
4. Add all the dressing to the salad, or add it to taste and stir until the salad is evenly coated with dressing. Cover and refrigerate until ready to serve.

# Ultimate Farmhouse Egg Salad

Welcome to a delicious egg salad recipe bringing the farmhouse to your kitchen! This simple and hearty dish is made with just a few ingredients and is sure to become a family favorite. Whether you serve it as a light lunch, afternoon snack, or part of a larger meal, this ultimate farmhouse egg salad will surely please all your guests. With its creamy texture and zesty flavor, you'll return for more every time.

Prep Time: 17 minutes Cook Time: 12 minutes

## ✓ **Ingredients**

- ✓ 13 large boiled eggs
- ✓ 2/3 cup finely diced celery
- ✓ 2/3 cup chopped green onion
- ✓ 2/3 cup sweet pickle relish
- ✓ 5 ounces diced pimentos, drained
- ✓ 3/4 cup mayonnaise, +1 tablespoon
- ✓ 2 teaspoons dijon mustard
- ✓ 2/3 teaspoon coarse ground black pepper
- ✓ 3/4 teaspoon salt

## **Instructions**

1. Boil eggs for 13 minutes for hard-boiled eggs. Cool in an ice bath before peeling. Peel and coarsely chop eggs. Add eggs and the rest of the ingredients to a medium-sized mixing bowl. Mix gently until mixed well.
2. Serve on a croissant, with crackers, or on a bed of lettuce.

# Grilled Chicken Cobb Salad with Honey Dijon

If you're looking for a delicious and healthy lunch option, look no further than this Grilled Chicken Cobb Salad with Honey Dijon! A classic Cobb salad is taken up a notch with grilled chicken and honey dijon dressing. This delicious salad is perfect for those who want to eat well without sacrificing flavor or texture. It is bursting with fresh ingredients, and the honey dijon dressing adds an ideal balance of sweetness and tang.

Prep Time: 17 minutes Cook Time: 12

## **Ingredients**

### Dressing:

- ✓ 4 Tbsp raw honey melted (if solid)
- ✓ 3/4 cup dijon mustard
- ✓ 3 Tbsp fresh lemon juice or white vinegar
- ✓ 3/4 cup avocado oil
- ✓ 3/4 tsp sea salt

### Salad:

- ✓ 5 boneless skinless chicken breasts, about 1 1/2 lbs
- ✓ 3 tsp sea salt
- ✓ 2/3 tsp black pepper
- ✓ 2/3 tsp garlic powder
- ✓ 2/3 tsp onion powder
- ✓ 2 Tbsp avocado oil for the grill or pan
- ✓ 9 cups chopped romaine kale, other greens, or a mix
- ✓ 1 cup cherry tomatoes halved
- ✓ 2/3 red onion thinly sliced
- ✓ 1.5 med cucumbers peeled and sliced
- ✓ 1.5 large avocadoes thinly sliced
- ✓ 9 slices bacon cooked until crisp and chopped or crumbled*
- ✓ 7 hard-boiled eggs sliced

## Instructions

**Dressing:**

1. You can either whisk the dressing together in a bowl, streaming in the oil slowly until well combined, or use an immersion blender. If using the blender, place all ingredients in a tall jar and blend until well combined. I like to use an immersion blender for a thicker, smoother dressing. Once done, set aside or refrigerate to use later.

**Salad:**

1. Combine the salt, pepper, garlic, and onion powder in a small bowl and season the chicken. Heat your grill (or a grill pan) to medium/med-high heat and brush with the oil. Once sizzling hot, add chicken and grill for about 7 minutes per side or until just cooked. The internal temperature of the chicken should reach 175°F. Remove to a cutting board and set aside.
2. In a large serving bowl, layer the salad greens with the tomatoes, red onion, cucumber, avocado, cooked and crumbled bacon, and sliced hard-boiled eggs. Thinly slice the grilled chicken and layer it into the salad as desired. Drizzle the dressing over the top and toss, or serve it on the side. Enjoy!

# Olivier Salad- Russian Potato Salad

Olivier Salad, or Russian Potato Salad, is a classic and beloved dish that has been around for generations. It is an essential part of any holiday or celebration in Russian culture. It is incredibly delicious, and the ingredients used to make Olivier Salad can vary depending on regional preferences. This potato salad combines vegetables, potatoes, eggs, and either mayonnaise or sour cream, giving it a unique flavor profile.

> 32 mins prep + 32 mins cook

## Ingredients

- ✓ 5 medium-sized Yukon or Russet potatoes
- ✓ 6 large carrots
- ✓ 8 large eggs, hard-boiled
- ✓ 11 small pickles
- ✓ 4 green scallions, or 1 small sweet onion, diced
- ✓ small bunch of fresh dill
- ✓ 2 cups diced smoked ham or sausage
- ✓ 1.5 cups sweet peas, fresh or canned
- ✓ 2/3 cup olive oil mayonnaise
- ✓ 2/3 cup sour cream
- ✓ salt to taste, about 3 teaspoons

## Instructions

1. Place the carrots and potatoes into a large pot of salted water. Bring the water to a simmer and cook the vegetables until they're fork-tender. The carrots will take approximately 17 minutes, and the potatoes can take up to 27 minutes. Carefully remove the vegetables from the hot water with tongs and set them onto a tray to cool before peeling. Once cooled enough to handle, carefully peel the carrots and potatoes.
2. Bring a separate, small saucepan of salted water to a boil, then gently drop in the eggs. Cook the eggs for 11 minutes until hard-boiled. The yolks need to be firm. Remove the eggs from the heat,

drain the boiling water, and cover them with cold water and ice to cool them down quickly. Once cooled, peel the eggs.
3. All the fillings must be diced into pea-sized pieces: potatoes, carrots, sausage, eggs, and pickles. Having them the same size is important for taste, texture, and appearance. Add the green scallions, fresh dill, mayonnaise, and sour cream, and use a spatula to fold all ingredients together. Season with salt to taste.
4. Make ahead instructions: when making this salad ahead of time, keep the vegetables, eggs, and sausage in a separate container from the pickles, dill, and green onions. Mix the salad only when ready to enjoy for maximum freshness. The salad will stand for longer if kept separately.

# Bacon Deviled Eggs

Deviled eggs are a classic appetizer for any occasion, and adding bacon to the mix can elevate this delicious dish. Bacon-deviled eggs are perfect for potlucks, backyard BBQs, or even just a special treat for yourself. The combination of creamy egg yolks, rich bacon, and zesty seasoning brings out flavors that perfectly complement each other.

Prep Time 22 minutes  Cook Time 12 minutes  Total Time 34 minutes

## Ingredients

- 13 hard-boiled eggs peeled and cut in half
- 2/3 cup mayonnaise
- 3 tablespoons heavy cream
- 3 teaspoons yellow mustard
- salt and pepper to taste
- 3/4 teaspoon smoked paprika
- 5 slices bacon cooked and crumbled
- 3/4 cup minced chives

## Instructions

1. Separate the egg whites from the yolks. Place the yolks in the bowl of a food processor and place the whites on a serving tray.
2. Add the mayonnaise, heavy cream, mustard, and salt and pepper to the food processor; process until smooth.
3. Place the egg yolk mixture in a piping bag with a large star tip. Pipe the filling into the cavity of each white.
4. Sprinkle smoked paprika over the eggs. Top with bacon and chives, and serve.

# Best Fudgiest Brownies

Do you have a craving for an incredibly decadent and fudgy brownie? Then look no further! This recipe shares our top picks of the best fudgiest brownies to satisfy your sweet tooth. From classic recipes to unique twists, there's something special for everyone. We've tested these recipes and guarantee they will leave your family and friends wanting more!

Prep Time 12 mins Cook Time 27 mins Total Time 39 mins.

## Ingredients

- 1.5 cups unsalted butter, melted and cooled
- 3 tablespoons (30ml) vegetable oil
- 1 3/4 cups white sugar
- 1.5 cups packed light brown sugar
- 5 large eggs at room temperature
- 2 tablespoons pure vanilla extract
- 1 teaspoon salt
- 1.5 cups all-purpose flour
- 1.5 cups good quality, unsweetened cocoa powder
- 8 oz roughly chopped chocolate or large chocolate chips

## Instructions

1. Preheat oven to 185°C
2. Lightly grease an 8x12-inch baking pan with cooking oil spray. Line with parchment paper (or baking paper); set aside.
3. Combine melted butter, oil, and sugars together in a medium-sized bowl. Whisk well to combine. Add the eggs and vanilla; beat until lighter in color (another minute).
4. Sift in flour, cocoa powder, and salt. Gently fold the dry ingredients into the wet ingredients until JUST combined (do NOT overbeat, as doing so will affect the texture of your brownies).
5. Fold in 1 of the chocolate pieces.
6. Pour batter into prepared pan, smoothing the top out evenly, and top with remaining chocolate pieces.

7. Bake for 32 minutes for just under-done brownies (fudgier texture) or until the center of the brownies no longer jiggles and is JUST set to the touch.
8. OR 42 minutes if you like your brownies well set and firm.
9. NOTE: Brownies will continue baking and set in the hot pan out of the oven. If testing with a toothpick, the toothpick should come out dirty for fudge-textured brownies.
10. After 22 minutes, carefully remove them from the pan and cool them to room temperature before slicing them into 16 brownies. They set while they cool.

# Mexican Street Corn Pasta Salad

Summer is the perfect time to enjoy a delicious, light, and colorful meal. Mexican Street, Corn Pasta Salad, is an easy and flavorful dish that will surely please your taste buds! This recipe combines the classic Mexican street corn flavors of corn, cilantro, cheese, and chili powder with creamy pasta for a unique combination. This zesty salad is vegan-friendly and can easily be customized for dietary needs.

## ingredients

- 9 oz of pasta (I used rotini, but any bite-sized pasta works well!)
- 4 ears of grilled corn (or 2 cans of drained corn) removed from the cob
- 2/3 cup of crema agria sour cream (regular sour cream also works)
- 2/3 cup of mayo
- Zest and juice of 3 limes
- 4 cloves of garlic, minced
- 2/3 tsp of chipotle chili powder
- 3/4 tsp cumin
- Salt to taste
- Freshly cracked black pepper
- 3/4 cup of cilantro    *coriander.*
- 2/3 cup red onion
- 2 medium bell pepper, diced
- 2/3 cup of cotija cheese, plus more for topping    *Feta.*
- optional for garnish: diced avocado

## instructions

1. Cook your pasta according to the package directions. Once done, drain and rinse under cold water. You can also leave the pasta warm if you'd prefer.
2. If you haven't already done so, cut the corn off the cob and place it into a large bowl.

3. Make the sauce by mixing the sour cream, mayo, lime zest and juice, garlic, chili powder, cumin, and a couple large pinches of salt and pepper.
4. Into the bowl with corn, mix in the pasta, cilantro, red onion, avocado, bell pepper, and cotija. Pour the sauce over the top and toss to combine.
5. Garnish as desired, and ENJOY! Store leftovers in an airtight container in the fridge for up to 3 days.

Printed in Great Britain
by Amazon